D1232617

To:

_____

From:

_____

HIS INDWELLING SPIRIT

WALKING WITH GOD VOLUME 2

QUOTATIONS FROM
DR. CHARLES F. STANLEY

THOMAS NELSON
Since 1798

NASHVILLE   MEXICO CITY   RIO DE JANEIRO

Published in Nashville, Tennessee, by Thomas Nelson. Thomas Nelson is a registered trademark of HarperCollins Christian Publishing, Inc.

Thomas Nelson titles may be purchased in bulk for educational, business, fund-raising, or sales promotional use. For information, please e-mail SpecialMarkets@ThomasNelson.com.

Unless otherwise noted, Scripture quotations are taken from the NEW AMERICAN STANDARD BIBLE®, Copyright ©1960, 1962, 1963, 1968, 1971, 1972, 1973, 1975, 1977, 1995 by The Lockman Foundation.

Scripture quotations marked NIV are taken from THE HOLY BIBLE, NEW INTERNATIONAL VERSION®, NIV® Copyright © 1973, 1978, 1984, 2011 by Biblica, Inc.™ Used by permission. All rights reserved worldwide.

Scripture quotations marked NKJV are taken from the NEW KING JAMES VERSION®. Copyright © 1982 by Thomas Nelson, Inc.

The following quotations have been taken from:

The sermons of Dr. Charles Stanley as they were preached at the First Baptist Church in Atlanta, Georgia, and may contain slight differences from the published audio or video series from which they were taken.

Charles F. Stanley's Handbook for Christian Living, copyright © 2008 by Charles F. Stanley. Published in Nashville, Tennessee, by Thomas Nelson, Inc.

Charles F. Stanley Life Principle Bible, copyright © 2009 by Charles F. Stanley. Published in Nashville, Tennessee, by Thomas Nelson, Inc.

Living in the Power of the Holy Spirit, copyright © 2005 by Charles F. Stanley. Published in Nashville, Tennessee, by Thomas Nelson, Inc.

The Ultimate Conversation, copyright © 2012 by Charles F. Stanley. Published in New York, New York, by Howard Books, a division of Simon & Schuster, Inc.

The Wonderful Spirit-Filled Life, copyright © 1992 by Charles Stanley. Published in Nashville, Tennessee, by Thomas Nelson, Inc.

ISBN-13: 978-0-529-10896-8

Printed in U.S.A.

15 16 17 18 19 20 RRD 6 5 4 3 2

TABLE OF CONTENTS

WHO HE IS

God in Three Persons,
Blessed Trinity

*There are three that bear witness in heaven: the Father, the Word,
and the Holy Spirit; and these three are one.*

—1 JOHN 5:7 NKJV

You can't receive just a part of God.
In receiving God the Son, you are
receiving the fullness of God into your
life. That person of God, who resides
within you—dwells in you, abides in you,
fills you—is the Holy Spirit. . . . He has
given us the fullness of His own nature
that we truly might be created anew
spiritually in His likeness.

DR. CHARLES F. STANLEY

From his book,
Living in the Power of the Holy Spirit

Of His fullness we have all received, and grace upon grace. For the
Law was given through Moses; grace and truth were realized through
Jesus Christ. No one has seen God at any time; the only begotten
God who is in the bosom of the Father, He has explained Him.
—JOHN 1:16–18

There are three persons of the Trinity. There is one Godhead—three persons. God the Father, Son, and Holy Spirit are intimately and actively involved with all creation. The Father does His work. The Son does His work. The Spirit does His work. Each has a vital role in every believer's life.

DR. CHARLES F. STANLEY

From his sermon,
"Walking in the Holy Spirit"
Life Principles to Live By

 To those . . . who are chosen according to the foreknowledge of God the Father, by the sanctifying work of the Spirit, to obey Jesus Christ and be sprinkled with His blood: May grace and peace be yours in the fullest measure.
—1 PETER 1:1–2

We don't worship three gods. We have one God who exists with three unique functions. The Father, the Son, and the Holy Spirit live in perfect agreement and oneness, with all the same attributes. Each is eternal, omnipotent, omniscient, omnipresent, unchanging, equal, and fully God.

DR. CHARLES F. STANLEY

From his sermon,
"The Truth About the Trinity"

 The grace of the Lord Jesus Christ, and the love of God, and the fellowship of the Holy Spirit, be with you all.
—2 CORINTHIANS 13:14

The Holy Spirit is not an apparition, floating about here and there and manifesting Himself in a mysterious, now-you-see-Him, now-you-don't manner. . . . The Holy Spirit is the living personhood of God . . . the full personality and identity of God resident in us as believers.

DR. CHARLES F. STANLEY

From his book,
Living in the Power of the Holy Spirit

 Who among men knows the thoughts of a man except the spirit of the man which is in him? Even so the thoughts of God no one knows except the Spirit of God.
—1 CORINTHIANS 2:11

We will never be able to grasp what God is like and who He really is until we understand the basics of what the Bible teaches about the Trinity. What an awesome blessing you and I have when we fully recognize that God is our heavenly Father, Jesus is our Savior and Lord, and the Holy Spirit is our great Helper and Empowerer.

DR. CHARLES F. STANLEY

From his sermon,
"The Truth About the Trinity"

Beloved, building yourselves up on your most holy faith, praying in the Holy Spirit, keep yourselves in the love of God, waiting anxiously for the mercy of our Lord Jesus Christ to eternal life.
—JUDE 20–21

The New Testament [is] consistent in its presentation of the Holy Spirit as a "He" rather than an "It." . . . He is a thinking, feeling, active person working with God the Father and God the Son to affect our lives according to their collective will.

DR. CHARLES F. STANLEY

From his book,
The Wonderful Spirit-Filled Life

"That is the Spirit of truth, whom the world cannot receive, because it does not see Him or know Him, but you know Him because He abides with you and will be in you."
—JOHN 14:17

The Holy Spirit is never the cause
of depression, stress, anxiety, or
confusion. He is always the solution
to those conditions.

DR. CHARLES F. STANLEY

From his book,
Living in the Power of the Holy Spirit

There is now no condemnation for those who are in Christ Jesus.
For the law of the Spirit of life in Christ Jesus has set you free from
the law of sin and of death.
—ROMANS 8:1–2

When Jesus mentions "another Helper," He uses the Greek word *allos*, which means "another of the same kind." Jesus promised He would send someone just like Him to be with us and love us just as He does. So the Holy Spirit's presence with us is an expression of God's love toward us.

DR. CHARLES F. STANLEY

From his sermon,
"God's Answer for Our Inadequacy"

 "I will ask the Father, and He will give you another Helper, that He may be with you forever."
—JOHN 14:16

The word "helper" is *parakletos*, which means, "one who walks alongside, assists us, and is our steadfast companion." Scripture teaches that every believer has a constant, unending, faithful companion—that is the person of the Holy Spirit.

DR. CHARLES F. STANLEY

From his sermon,
"Our Constant Companion"

"The Helper, the Holy Spirit, whom the Father will send in My name, He will teach you all things, and bring to your remembrance all that I said to you."
—JOHN 14:26

The Holy Spirit is not a force. He is as much a person as Jesus is. He is the One who walks beside us, our Helper and Comforter. He is the One who gives us assurance of our relationships to the Father. He testifies to each believer, "You are one of God's children. You have been adopted into the kingdom forever."

DR. CHARLES F. STANLEY

From his sermon,
"Walking in the Holy Spirit"
Life Principles to Live By

 The Spirit Himself testifies with our spirit
that we are children of God.
—ROMANS 8:16

We are limited by time. We see only today and can only guess about tomorrow. But when God works in your life, He knows all things, sees all of your days, is present everywhere, has all power, and is not hindered by earthly limitations as we are. All three persons of the Godhead—the Father, Son, and Holy Spirit—work in cooperation to accomplish His plans for your life with full knowledge of your past, your todays, and your tomorrows.

DR. CHARLES F. STANLEY

From his sermon,
"The Trinity"

 LORD, You have been our dwelling place in all generations. Before the mountains were born or You gave birth to the earth and the world, even from everlasting to everlasting, You are God. . . . So teach us to number our days, that we may present to You a heart of wisdom.
—PSALM 90:1–2, 12

Many people seem to think that the Holy Spirit has only been poured out on those who are preachers, teachers, missionaries, or some other type of full-time Christian worker. Not so! The anointing power of the Holy Spirit is for every believer.

DR. CHARLES F. STANLEY

From his book,
Living in the Power of the Holy Spirit

We should always give thanks to God for you, brethren beloved by the Lord, because God has chosen you from the beginning for salvation through sanctification by the Spirit and faith in the truth.
—2 THESSALONIANS 2:13

I think one of the primary reasons the church is so weak today is that we don't understand who the Holy Spirit is. He's some cloud, some vapor, some nondescript power; and we don't know how He relates to us. But He is the very power of God living within us—enabling us to do what we would never be able to do apart from a personal experience with Him.

DR. CHARLES F. STANLEY

From his sermon,
"The Holy Spirit—His True Identity"
The Power of the Holy Spirit in the Life of the Believer

"You will receive power when the Holy Spirit has come upon you; and you shall be My witnesses both in Jerusalem, and in all Judea and Samaria, and even to the remotest part of the earth."
—ACTS 1:8

It is the Holy Spirit's job—*not ours*—
to convict people of their sin.

DR. CHARLES F. STANLEY

From
The Charles F. Stanley Life Principles Bible

I know my transgressions, and my sin is ever before me. Against You,
You only, I have sinned and done what is evil in Your sight, so that
You are justified when You speak and blameless when You judge.
—PSALM 51:3–4

The Holy Spirit is a vital part of everything in the Word of God—including the very inspiration of the Word itself.

DR. CHARLES F. STANLEY

From his sermon,
"The Mission of the Spirit"
Living in the Power of the Holy Spirit

 "The Spirit of the LORD spoke by me, and
His word was on my tongue."
—2 SAMUEL 23:2

If you want to know what the Holy Spirit
thinks about something, read the Bible.
The Scripture is His thoughts on paper.

DR. CHARLES F. STANLEY

From his book,
The Wonderful Spirit-Filled Life

 All Scripture is inspired by God and profitable for teaching, for
reproof, for correction, for training in righteousness; so that the man
of God may be adequate, equipped for every good work.
—2 TIMOTHY 3:16–17

The Bible . . . ascribes to Him all the distinctives of personality. Specifically, the Holy Spirit is described as having (1) knowledge, (2) will, and (3) emotion. . . He is not a power to be harnessed and manipulated. He has a mind and will of His own. To tap into the Holy Spirit is not to enhance one's ability to carry out one's will. Oh no! On the contrary, the power of the Holy Spirit is available only to those whose intention is to carry out His will.

DR. CHARLES F. STANLEY

From his book,
The Wonderful Spirit-Filled Life

 One and the same Spirit works all these things, distributing to each one individually just as He wills.
—1 CORINTHIANS 12:11

The Holy Spirit is God. The Holy Spirit lives in me—permanently.

DR. CHARLES F. STANLEY

From his book,
The Wonderful Spirit-Filled Life

 Do you not know that you are a temple of God and that the Spirit of God dwells in you?
—1 CORINTHIANS 3:16

The Holy Spirit is God's assurance that our salvation is secure—it is promised to us for all eternity.

DR. CHARLES F. STANLEY

From his book,
Living in the Power of the Holy Spirit

He who establishes us with you in Christ and anointed us is God, who
also sealed us and gave us the Spirit in our hearts as a pledge.
—2 CORINTHIANS 1:21–22

The Holy Spirit is a vitally important part of your life. Why? The Father is in heaven as your Creator and Sovereign King, ruling all creation. Jesus is seated at His right hand, making intercession for you as Your Savior, Lord, and Advocate. But the Holy Spirit is here living within you. He is your Helper, Anointer, Encourager, and Comforter. He is the One living within you, enabling you to be all God wants you to be.

DR. CHARLES F. STANLEY

From his sermon,
"Our Constant Companion"

May the God of peace Himself sanctify you entirely; and may your spirit and soul and body be preserved complete, without blame at the coming of our Lord Jesus Christ. Faithful is He who calls you, and He also will bring it to pass.
—1 THESSALONIANS 5:23–24

If we go through our lives neglecting
and ignoring the person and the work of
the Holy Spirit, we're going to be losers
because we will never experience the
awesome victory God has for us—the
triumph that can only come if we walk in
the power of the Holy Spirit.

DR. CHARLES F. STANLEY

From his sermon,
"The Promise of the Father"
Living in the Power of the Holy Spirit

My message and my preaching were not in persuasive words of wisdom,
but in demonstration of the Spirit and of power, so that your faith
would not rest on the wisdom of men, but on the power of God.
—1 CORINTHIANS 2:4–5

The Holy Spirit is God's seal of ownership
on us throughout eternity. He claims us
forever as His children, and our redemption
brings Him praise and glory.

DR. CHARLES F. STANLEY

From his sermon,
"The Promise of the Father"
Living in the Power of the Holy Spirit

 What is mortal will be swallowed up by life. Now He who prepared us
for this very purpose is God, who gave to us the Spirit as a pledge.
—2 CORINTHIANS 5:4–5

Blasphemy against the Spirit is
unforgivable because it means denying
Jesus Christ is who He says He is and
denying His gift of salvation.

DR. CHARLES F. STANLEY

From
The Charles F. Stanley Life Principles Bible

"Any sin and blasphemy shall be forgiven people, but blasphemy against
the Spirit shall not be forgiven. Whoever speaks a word against the Son of
Man, it shall be forgiven him; but whoever speaks against the Holy Spirit,
it shall not be forgiven him, either in this age or in the age to come."
—MATTHEW 12:31–32

The Holy Spirit is a change agent. . . . Radical change is possible. We have everything we need to become all He wants us to become.

DR. CHARLES F. STANLEY

From his book,
The Wonderful Spirit-Filled Life

 His divine power has granted to us everything pertaining to life and godliness, through the true knowledge of Him who called us by His own glory and excellence.
—2 PETER 1:3

WHAT HE DOES

Leading Us from
Glory to Glory

*We all, with unveiled face, beholding as in a mirror the glory of
the Lord, are being transformed into the same image from glory to
glory, just as from the Lord, the Spirit.*

—2 CORINTHIANS 3:18

The only way to be saved is by the Holy Spirit convicting you of sin, giving you the gift of faith, and showing you the truth. You accept the message of the gospel of Jesus Christ, and God transforms your life through the power of the Holy Spirit.

DR. CHARLES F. STANLEY

From his sermon,
"Our Constant Companion"

 Jesus answered, "Truly, truly, I say to you,
unless one is born of water and the Spirit he
cannot enter into the kingdom of God."
—JOHN 3:5

We are saved by the grace of God—the grace provided by the Father in heaven, by the Son at His crucifixion, and by the power of the Holy Spirit here on earth whereby He convicts us of our need for salvation.

DR. CHARLES F. STANLEY

From his sermon,
"The Trinity"

 Grace to you and peace, from Him who is and who was and who is to come.
—REVELATION 1:4

There is only one requirement for
receiving the Holy Spirit into your
life and that is believing.

DR. CHARLES F. STANLEY

From his book,
Living in the Power of the Holy Spirit

Peter said to them, "Repent, and each of you be baptized in
the name of Jesus Christ for the forgiveness of your sins;
and you will receive the gift of the Holy Spirit."
—ACTS 2:38

The baptism of the Holy Spirit is His work at your salvation when He places you in Jesus and makes you a permanent part of the whole body of Christ.

DR. CHARLES F. STANLEY

From his sermon,
"The Holy Spirit—An Absolute Essential"

By one Spirit we were all baptized into one body, whether Jews or Greeks, whether slaves or free, and we were all made to drink of one Spirit.
—1 CORINTHIANS 12:13

The Holy Spirit takes up residency in believers—forever. He doesn't just pass through. He makes us His home. He comes to stay.

DR. CHARLES F. STANLEY

From his book,
The Wonderful Spirit-Filled Life

 Do you not know that your body is a temple of the Holy Spirit who is in you, whom you have from God, and that you are not your own? For you have been bought with a price: therefore glorify God in your body.
—1 CORINTHIANS 6:19–20

Receiving the Holy Spirit is a onetime event—we receive the Holy Spirit when we receive Christ as our Savior. . . . The decision to grow and to keep on growing is a decision that we must continue to make every day of our lives. We must choose to be filled with the Holy Spirit each and every day.

DR. CHARLES F. STANLEY

From his book,
Living in the Power of the Holy Spirit

For this reason also, since the day we heard of it, we have not ceased to pray for you and to ask that you may be filled with the knowledge of His will in all spiritual wisdom and understanding, so that you will walk in a manner worthy of the Lord, to please Him in all respects, bearing fruit in every good work and increasing in the knowledge of God.
—COLOSSIANS 1:9–10

The power of the Holy Spirit is the divine authority and energy that God releases into the life of every one of His children in order that we might live godly and fruitful lives.

DR. CHARLES F. STANLEY

From his book,
Living in the Power of the Holy Spirit

 "Abide in Me, and I in you. As the branch cannot bear fruit of itself unless it abides in the vine, so neither can you unless you abide in Me."
—JOHN 15:4

Within the eternal fellowship of the Trinity, the members of the Godhead have always enjoyed a deep, rich, and unbroken relationship of love with one another. When God created us, He wanted us to share in some measure of that fellowship; that's why He created us in His image. By creating us to reflect His own nature, He made it possible for us to develop a deep and intimate relationship with Himself.

DR. CHARLES F. STANLEY

From
The Charles F. Stanley Life Principles Bible

 God said, "Let Us make man in Our image, according to Our likeness . . .God created man in His own image, in the image of God He created him; male and female He created them."
—GENESIS 1:26–27

One of the primary reasons God sent the Holy Spirit is to lead us to a life of fulfillment. That is, so you and I could live the kind of life that bears the characteristics of Jesus.

DR. CHARLES F. STANLEY

From his sermon,
"Our Constant Companion"

 The fruit of the Spirit is love, joy, peace, patience, kindness, goodness, faithfulness, gentleness, self-control; against such things there is no law.
—GALATIANS 5:22–23

The promise of a Helper was Jesus' way of tipping us off to one of the most profound truths concerning the Christian life—it's impossible! The quality of life Jesus expects from His followers is unattainable apart from outside intervention.

DR. CHARLES F. STANLEY

From his book,
The Wonderful Spirit-Filled Life

 "I tell you the truth, it is to your advantage that I go away; for if I do not go away, the Helper will not come to you; but if I go, I will send Him to you."
—JOHN 16:7

The power of the Holy Spirit was given
for a very specific purpose—to enable us to
be witnesses for Jesus Christ.

DR. CHARLES F. STANLEY

From his book,
The Wonderful Spirit-Filled Life

 "When they bring you before the synagogues and the rulers and
the authorities, do not worry about how or what you are to speak
in your defense, or what you are to say; for the Holy Spirit will
teach you in that very hour what you ought to say."
—LUKE 12:11–12

The entire world has been impacted by the gospel of Jesus Christ. It started with one Man, then eleven, then one hundred and twenty, and then three thousand—and on it went. You know why it worked? Simply because it was the work of the Spirit of God, not the efforts of man.

DR. CHARLES F. STANLEY

From his sermon,
"Our Constant Companion"

 "Know for certain that God has made Him both Lord and Christ—this Jesus whom you crucified." Now when they heard this, they were pierced to the heart . . . and that day there were added about three thousand souls.
—ACTS 2:36–37, 41

The Holy Spirit manifests His power in whatever way He deems necessary to enable believers to be effective witnesses for Christ.

DR. CHARLES F. STANLEY

From his book,
The Wonderful Spirit-Filled Life

"Go therefore and make disciples of all the nations, baptizing them in the name of the Father and the Son and the Holy Spirit, teaching them to observe all that I commanded you; and lo, I am with you always, even to the end of the age."
—MATTHEW 28:19–20

It is the authority, power, and unction
of the Holy Spirit that teaches through a
Sunday school teacher, pastor, musician, or
evangelist. God intends for all of us to do
our work in His wisdom, energy,
strength, and by His authority.

DR. CHARLES F. STANLEY

From his sermon,
"Walking in the Holy Spirit"
Life Principles to Live By

"When the Helper comes, whom I will send to you from the
Father, that is the Spirit of truth who proceeds from the
Father, He will testify about Me, and you will testify also,
because you have been with Me from the beginning."
—JOHN 15:26–27

Why did God send the Holy Spirit? Simply because He is ready, willing, and able to help you accomplish all that the Father has planned for you and to help you become the person He created you to be.

DR. CHARLES F. STANLEY

From his sermon,
"Our Constant Companion"

 Teach me to do Your will, for You are my God; let
Your good Spirit lead me on level ground.
—PSALM 143:10

The Spirit of truth is like an inner compass in our lives—always pointing us toward what Jesus would be, say, or do in any given moment.

DR. CHARLES F. STANLEY

From
The Charles F. Stanley Life Principles Bible

"We must obey God rather than men. The God of our fathers raised up Jesus, whom you had put to death by hanging Him on a cross. He is the one whom God exalted to His right hand as a Prince and a Savior, to grant repentance to Israel, and forgiveness of sins. And we are witnesses of these things; and so is the Holy Spirit, whom God has given to those who obey Him."
—ACTS 5:29–32

The Helper sees the depths of your difficulties. He translates your feelings more accurately than you could articulate them yourself. And He comforts you with the knowledge that He understands what you need.

DR. CHARLES F. STANLEY

From his book,
The Ultimate Conversation

 The Spirit also helps our weakness; for we do not know how to pray as we should, but the Spirit Himself intercedes for us with groanings too deep for words. —ROMANS 8:26

The Holy Spirit of the living God loves you so much—not because you're good, but because it is who He is. He's right there with you, no matter what happens.

DR. CHARLES F. STANLEY

From his sermon,
"Our Constant Companion"

 "The Lord is the one who goes ahead of you; He will be with you. He will not fail you or forsake you. Do not fear or be dismayed." —DEUTERONOMY 31:8

We bear the image of God, which is the capacity to possess knowledge. The image of God in us is the capacity to feel, have emotion, and to make decisions. But what identifies us as believers is that we have the Spirit of God indwelling us, making us holy, separating us, leading us, and distinguishing us from the rest of the world.

DR. CHARLES F. STANLEY

From his sermon,
"The Holy Spirit—His True Identity"
The Power of the Holy Spirit in the Life of the Believer

This is what we speak, not in words taught us by human wisdom but in words taught by the Spirit, expressing spiritual truths in spiritual words.
—1 CORINTHIANS 2:13

The Holy Spirit *knows* the thoughts of God. And He imparts [that] knowledge to believers.

DR. CHARLES F. STANLEY

From his book,
The Wonderful Spirit-Filled Life

 We have received, not the spirit of the world, but the Spirit who is from God, so that we may know the things freely given to us by God.
—1 CORINTHIANS 2:12

The Helper . . . faithfully conveys to us the Father's will in a way we understand, and He represents us before God in a manner worthy of His righteous name. . . . You should never fear whether God will acknowledge the cries of your heart, because His Holy Spirit transforms your petitions into acceptable and pleasing sacrifices.

DR. CHARLES F. STANLEY

From his book,
The Ultimate Conversation

Let the words of my mouth and the meditation
of my heart be acceptable in Your sight, O LORD,
my rock and my Redeemer.
—PSALM 19:14

No one knows us like the Spirit of God knows us.

DR. CHARLES F. STANLEY

From his sermon,
"Your Spiritual Growth"

 Search me, O God, and know my heart; try me and know
my anxious thoughts; and see if there be any hurtful way
in me, and lead me in the everlasting way.
—PSALM 139:23–24

The presence of the Holy Spirit is a spiritual reminder of God's promise to finish what He has begun in you.

DR. CHARLES F. STANLEY

From his book,
The Wonderful Spirit-Filled Life

I am confident of this very thing, that He
who began a good work in you will perfect it
until the day of Christ Jesus.
—PHILIPPIANS 1:6

The Holy Spirit is a wonderful communicator. But He does not speak for the purpose of passing along information. He speaks to get a response. . . . He waits for us to become neutral enough to hear and eventually obey.

DR. CHARLES F. STANLEY

From his book,
The Wonderful Spirit-Filled Life

"Obey My voice, and I will be your God, and you will be My people; and you will walk in all the way which I command you, that it may be well with you."
—JEREMIAH 7:23

The Holy Spirit is the Teacher; I'm just a mouthpiece for the truth.

DR. CHARLES F. STANLEY

From his sermon,
"The Mission of the Spirit"
Living in the Power of the Holy Spirit

 "My Spirit which is upon you, and My words which I have put
in your mouth shall not depart from your mouth, nor from the
mouth of your offspring, nor from the mouth of your
offspring's offspring," says the LORD, "from now and forever."
—ISAIAH 59:21

The Holy Spirit strengthens your intimacy with the Father by continually drawing you into His presence. However, He does not usher you to the throne of grace simply so you can give the Lord a list of demands. He is there to deepen your relationship. This means He encourages you to share your heart with God but also directs you to pay attention to what the Father is teaching you.

DR. CHARLES F. STANLEY

From his book,
The Ultimate Conversation

Guard your steps as you go to the house of God and draw near to listen rather than to offer the sacrifice of fools; for they do not know they are doing evil. Do not be hasty in word or impulsive in thought to bring up a matter in the presence of God. For God is in heaven and you are on the earth; therefore let your words be few.
—ECCLESIASTES 5:1–2

When you begin looking for the Holy Spirit, when you begin tuning in to the absence or presence of His peace, you are going to be overwhelmed by the consistency of His presence. You are going to be amazed at His willingness to lead. And best of all, you are going to be assured of the love of your heavenly Father. It is a love that reaches into every detail of your life.

DR. CHARLES F. STANLEY

From his book,
The Wonderful Spirit-Filled Life

 May the God of hope fill you with all joy and peace in believing, so that you will abound in hope by the power of the Holy Spirit. —ROMANS 15:13

Faith is the Holy Spirit's signal to go into action.

DR. CHARLES F. STANLEY

From his book,
The Wonderful Spirit-Filled Life

Without faith it is impossible to please Him, for he who
comes to God must believe that He is and that He is a
rewarder of those who seek Him.
—HEBREWS 11:6

The mark of the Holy Spirit is not excitement or crowds. When the Holy Spirit has been part of something, you will always find fruit, character, restored relationships, and men and women whose lives radiate the love of Christ.

DR. CHARLES F. STANLEY

From his book,
The Wonderful Spirit-Filled Life

 The wisdom from above is first pure, then peaceable, gentle, reasonable, full of mercy and good fruits, unwavering, without hypocrisy. And the seed whose fruit is righteousness is sown in peace by those who make peace.
—JAMES 3:17–18

God's ultimate goal for man necessitates that His work be done in the Spirit. He is out to alter the heart of man, to bring about a renewal from the inside out. That cannot be done apart from the influence of the Holy Spirit.

DR. CHARLES F. STANLEY

From his book,
The Wonderful Spirit-Filled Life

"Moreover, I will give you a new heart and put a new spirit within you; and I will remove the heart of stone from your flesh and give you a heart of flesh. I will put My Spirit within you and cause you to walk in My statutes, and you will be careful to observe My ordinances."
—EZEKIEL 36:26–27

WHY WE NEED HIM

Imbuing Us with Power

I am filled with power—with the Spirit of the
LORD—and with justice and courage.

—MICAH 3:8

Within you is a person more powerful than any of the forces in the world. He is divine. He is eternal. He is the Holy Spirit. And He dwells within you to enable you for all God has planned.

DR. CHARLES F. STANLEY

From his sermon,
"Our Constant Companion"

 "Not by might nor by power, but by My Spirit," says the LORD of hosts.
—ZECHARIAH 4:6

You were saved because God's
Holy Spirit moved in you, opened your
blind eyes, exposed the Word of God to you,
and gave you enough truth by which
you could be saved.

DR. CHARLES F. STANLEY

From his sermon,
"The Trinity"

"No one can come to Me unless the
Father who sent Me draws him."
—JOHN 6:44

The Christian life is serious business.
You cannot live it apart from the
work of the Holy Spirit.

DR. CHARLES F. STANLEY

From his sermon,
"Listening to God—Walking with God"
Life Principles to Live By

 "Whoever believes in me, as Scripture has said, streams of
living water will flow from within him." By this he meant the
Spirit, whom those who believed in him were later to receive.
—JOHN 7:38–39 NIV

If the eleven men who had walked and talked with Jesus needed the Holy Spirit, how much more do we need Him?

DR. CHARLES F. STANLEY

From his book,
The Wonderful Spirit-Filled Life

Gathering them together, He commanded them not to leave Jerusalem, but to wait for what the Father had promised, "Which," He said, "you heard of from Me; for John baptized with water, but you will be baptized with the Holy Spirit not many days from now."
—ACTS 1:4–5

The Bible distinguishes between believers and unbelievers as those who are indwelt by the Spirit and those who are not. Not by conduct, though that's important. Not by behavior, though that's important. But we are either sealed and indwelt by the Holy Spirit, or we are not.

DR. CHARLES F. STANLEY

From his sermon,
"The Holy Spirit, An Absolute Essential"

 The firm foundation of God stands, having this seal, "The Lord knows those who are His."
—2 TIMOTHY 2:19

The Holy Spirit gives us a "want to" desire—
not just a "have to" obligation—to live a holy
life. We are holy because He is holy.

DR. CHARLES F. STANLEY

From his book,
Living in the Power of the Holy Spirit

 "Blessed are those who hunger and thirst for
righteousness, for they shall be satisfied."
—MATTHEW 5:6

If we say yes to the Holy Spirit, He always says yes to us. He works in us to the extent we allow His power to infuse us and His authority to be established over us.

DR. CHARLES F. STANLEY

From his book,
Living in the Power of the Holy Spirit

 Trust in the LORD with all your heart and do not lean on your own understanding. In all your ways acknowledge Him, and He will make your paths straight.
—PROVERBS 3:5–6

I knew that if I was going to preach the gospel there had to be more to me than just knowledge, wisdom, understanding, and experience. There had to be the power of God. There had to be an anointing by the Spirit of God, or it wasn't going to work—it wasn't going to transform people's lives.

DR. CHARLES F. STANLEY

From his sermon,
"Our Constant Companion"

With great power the apostles were giving testimony to the resurrection of the Lord Jesus, and abundant grace was upon them all.
—ACTS 4:33

You cannot interpret the Word of God
properly, you cannot live a godly life,
and you cannot serve the Lord adequately
apart from the power of the
Holy Spirit working in you.

DR. CHARLES F. STANLEY

From his sermon,
"Walking in the Holy Spirit"
Life Principles to Live By

 To us God revealed them through the Spirit; for the
Spirit searches all things, even the depths of God.
—1 CORINTHIANS 2:10

None of us can do the ministry God gives us on our own. That is part of God's plan. We must have His Holy Spirit at work in us.

DR. CHARLES F. STANLEY

From his book,
Living in the Power of the Holy Spirit

"I am sending forth the promise of My Father upon you; but you are to stay in the city until you are clothed with power from on high."
—LUKE 24:49

Jesus doesn't stop with calling on us to love our neighbors. He calls on us to love our enemies as well. This is a supernatural calling, and we must rely on the Holy Spirit to give us the capacity to love them.

DR. CHARLES F. STANLEY

From his book,
Charles F. Stanley's Handbook for Christian Living

"Love your enemies, and do good, and lend, expecting nothing in return; and your reward will be great, and you will be sons of the Most High; for He Himself is kind to ungrateful and evil men."
—LUKE 6:35

When you confront others with the gospel of Jesus Christ, the Spirit of God speaks through you, taking the Word of God and illuminating their minds to understand the truth. He convicts them of their sin, shows them that the death of Christ was for their forgiveness, and grants them the gift of faith through which they receive Jesus as their personal Savior and Lord. It is not up to you to convince anyone. It is God's supernatural work in them that does so.

DR. CHARLES F. STANLEY

From his sermon,
"The Holy Spirit in the Life of the Believer"

Christ did not send me to baptize, but to preach the gospel, not in cleverness of speech, so that the cross of Christ would not be made void. For the word of the cross is foolishness to those who are perishing, but to us who are being saved it is the power of God.
—1 CORINTHIANS 1:17–18

The Holy Spirit in you says, "You can" in every situation where you might otherwise say, "I can't."

DR. CHARLES F. STANLEY

From his book,
Living in the Power of the Holy Spirit

The angel answered and said to her, "The Holy Spirit will come upon you, and the power of the Most High will overshadow you; and for that reason the holy Child shall be called the Son of God. . . . For nothing will be impossible with God." And Mary said, "Behold, the bondslave of the Lord; may it be done to me according to your word." And the angel departed from her.
—LUKE 1:35, 37–38

There are times when only God can help us. There are situations that hurt so badly, no one else can possibly soothe our pain. There are circumstances when the sorrow is so deep and so overwhelming that no one can drag us out of it but Him. He is our Helper, and He knows exactly how to care for us.

DR. CHARLES F. STANLEY

From his sermon,
"The Promise of the Father"
Living in the Power of the Holy Spirit

You have turned for me my mourning into dancing; You have loosed my sackcloth and girded me with gladness, that my soul may sing praise to You and not be silent. O LORD my God, I will give thanks to You forever.
—PSALM 30:11–12

True peace does not merely dull our pain. A person who has genuine, godly peace can endure an avalanche of hardship and difficulty and still enjoy an inner peace that surpasses all human understanding. Why? Because it does not come from pleasant circumstances, nice events, or good things others may do for us. Instead, it is based on the fact that the Spirit of our holy, omnipotent, and never-changing God lives within us.

DR. CHARLES F. STANLEY

From
The Charles F. Stanley Life Principles Bible

"The steadfast of mind You will keep in perfect peace, because he trusts in You. Trust in the LORD forever, for in God the LORD, we have an everlasting Rock."
—ISAIAH 26:3–4

You and I are most like Christ when we totally surrender to the Holy Spirit—allowing Him to live, speak, and work through us.

DR. CHARLES F. STANLEY

From his sermon,
"Our Constant Companion"

I urge you, brethren, by the mercies of God, to present your bodies a living and holy sacrifice, acceptable to God, which is your spiritual service of worship.
—ROMANS 12:1

We never spiritually outgrow our dependency upon the Holy Spirit. The exact opposite is true. The more mature we are in our faith and the more intimate our relationship with our heavenly Father, the more dependent we must be on the Holy Spirit.

DR. CHARLES F. STANLEY

From his book,
Living in the Power of the Holy Spirit

The spiritual is not first, but the natural; then the spiritual. The first man is from the earth, earthy; the second man is from heaven. As is the earthy, so also are those who are earthy; and as is the heavenly, so also are those who are heavenly. Just as we have borne the image of the earthy, we will also bear the image of the heavenly.
—1 CORINTHIANS 15:46–49

Once you trust Christ as your Savior, you can never be lost. You can never lose your salvation because you were sealed by the Spirit of God. You aren't guaranteed eternal life by some preacher, doctrine, or theology. You are promised by a person of the Trinity—the Holy Spirit seals you forever as a child of God.

DR. CHARLES F. STANLEY

From his sermon,
"Our Constant Companion"

 After listening to the message of truth, the gospel of your salvation—having also believed, you were sealed in Him with the Holy Spirit of promise.
—EPHESIANS 1:13

It is just as important for a mother to be filled with the Holy Spirit and to be godly—to be an example to her children, grandchildren, and husband—as it is for a pastor to be filled with the Spirit to preach the gospel. The truth is, we cannot be what we ought to be apart from Him.

DR. CHARLES F. STANLEY

From his sermon,
"Our Constant Companion"

Your adornment must not be merely external . . . but let it be the hidden person of the heart, with the imperishable quality of a gentle and quiet spirit, which is precious in the sight of God.
—1 PETER 3:3–4

You should never feel like you're alone. Why? Simply because you're not! Once you trust Jesus Christ as your personal Savior, the Holy Spirit seals you in Him. You will never walk alone, work alone, live alone, or die alone. You have Him for all eternity.

DR. CHARLES F. STANLEY

From his sermon,
"Our Constant Companion"

 "I will not leave you as orphans; I will come to you." —JOHN 14:18

God would not indwell you if He did not intend for you to do something in your life for His sake. He intends to work through you to accomplish His purposes on this earth. God gives you His supernatural power in order to do supernatural work . . . so that you may participate fully and successfully in His divine plan.

DR. CHARLES F. STANLEY

From his book,
Living in the Power of the Holy Spirit

"You are My servant, I have chosen you and not rejected you. Do not fear, for I am with you; do not anxiously look about you, for I am your God. I will strengthen you, surely I will help you, surely I will uphold you with My righteous right hand."
—ISAIAH 41:9–10

The heart that is led by God's Spirit and filled with His truth is pleasing to Him—and the only one actually equipped to really adore Him.

DR. CHARLES F. STANLEY

From
The Charles F. Stanley Life Principles Bible

"True worshipers will worship the Father in spirit and truth; for such people the Father seeks to be His worshipers. God is spirit, and those who worship Him must worship in spirit and truth."
—JOHN 4:23–24

It is only as we allow the Holy Spirit to do His work in us—opening ourselves continually to His power and presence—that our very nature is transformed until we develop a character and a quality of personality that is loving, joyful, peaceful, patient, kind, good, faithful, gentle, and under control in all situations, with all people, at all times.

DR. CHARLES F. STANLEY

From his book,
Living in the Power of the Holy Spirit

You also became imitators of us and of the Lord, having received the word in much tribulation with the joy of the Holy Spirit, so that you became an example to all the believers. —1 THESSALONIANS 1:6–7

The Holy Spirit never gives up on us. He continues to convict, regenerate, comfort, teach, and guide us—with an insistent, compelling urgency.

DR. CHARLES F. STANLEY

From his book,
Living in the Power of the Holy Spirit

 "The LORD will not abandon His people on account of His great name, because the LORD has been pleased to make you a people for Himself."
—1 SAMUEL 12:22

No wonder our lives are characterized by defeat rather than victory; sorrow rather than joy; frustration rather than peace. Apart from the Helper, life is reduced to doing the best we can. And I don't know about you, but for me, that's not very good.

DR. CHARLES F. STANLEY

From his book,
The Wonderful Spirit-Filled Life

 It is God who is at work in you, both to will and to work for His good pleasure.
—PHILIPPIANS 2:13

It's the vine that does the work. The fruit is
a product of the sap that runs from the vine
into the branch. I couldn't get over the fact
that the Holy Spirit was willing and able to
produce through me the very fruit I had been
trying so hard to produce on my own.

DR. CHARLES F. STANLEY

From his book,
The Wonderful Spirit-Filled Life

 "I am the vine, you are the branches; he who
abides in Me and I in him, he bears much
fruit, for apart from Me you can do nothing."
—JOHN 15:5

Christ is our life. When the Holy Spirit takes up residency in us, He brings with Him an inexhaustible source of life. . . . The practical outworking of this is twofold: (1) personal victory over sin and (2) Spirit-energized service. God never intended for His children to live defeated lives.

DR. CHARLES F. STANLEY

From his book,
The Wonderful Spirit-Filled Life

 "It is the Spirit who gives life; the flesh profits nothing; the words that I have spoken to you are spirit and are life." —JOHN 6:63

The only way for you to know the mind of God is through Scripture and the indwelling presence of the Holy Spirit. Through Scripture, the Holy Spirit sifts out, purifies, and clarifies your thinking process so you are able to think as God would have you to.

DR. CHARLES F. STANLEY

From his book,
Charles F. Stanley's Handbook for Christian Living

 He who is spiritual appraises all things . . .
We have the mind of Christ.
—1 CORINTHIANS 2:15–16

WHERE HE PROTECTS US

Strengthening Our Inner Being

I pray that out of His glorious riches He may strengthen you with power through His Spirit in your inner being.

—EPHESIANS 3:16 NIV

Everything in our lives that is not of God separates us—to some degree—from His work, will, purpose, and plan. The Holy Spirit convicts us of these things so we will let go of them and cling to Him. Then He can accomplish what is absolutely impossible any other way. You see, not a single one of us knows what our potential is—but He does. And He wants to see it accomplished in us.

DR. CHARLES F. STANLEY

From his sermon,
"The Holy Spirit—His True Identity"
The Power of the Holy Spirit in the Life of the Believer

 Let us throw off everything that hinders and the sin that so easily entangles, and let us run with perseverance the race marked out for us.
—HEBREWS 12:1 NIV

Every morning, you wake up to three enemies—the world, the flesh, and the Devil. How do you handle these enemies? You must be filled with the Holy Spirit—listening to and walking with Him moment by moment.

DR. CHARLES F. STANLEY

From his sermon,
"Walking in the Holy Spirit"
Life Principles to Live By

 For though we walk in the flesh, we do not war according to the flesh, for the weapons of our warfare are not of the flesh, but divinely powerful for the destruction of fortresses.
—2 CORINTHIANS 10:3–4

The tendency within us is to rebel against God, to want our way versus His way, and to yield to temptation. But when we walk in the Spirit, surrendered to His prevailing control, He helps us to stand strong against sin.

DR. CHARLES F. STANLEY

From his sermon,
"The Holy Spirit—An Absolute Essential"

 Walk by the Spirit, and you will not carry out the desire of the flesh. —GALATIANS 5:16

Jesus triumphed over Satan at the Cross—a victory that contained absolutely no hint of defeat. You also can claim victory over the enemy in daily battles because, as a believer, you are indwelt with the triumphant power of Jesus Christ through the presence of the Holy Spirit. You have the privilege of calling upon the divine power of God, which ultimately means you have authority over Satan and all his demons.

DR. CHARLES F. STANLEY

From
The Charles F. Stanley Life Principles Bible

 You are from God, little children, and have overcome them; because greater is He who is in you than he who is in the world.
—1 JOHN 4:4

As you study Scripture, the Holy Spirit works on you, increasing your discomfort in the areas you are withholding from Him. He also brings to mind the things you've learned, with the goal of helping you find freedom from any bondage that remains in your life.

DR. CHARLES F. STANLEY

From his book,
The Ultimate Conversation

 I acknowledged my sin to You, and my iniquity I did not hide; I said, "I will confess my transgressions to the LORD"; and You forgave the guilt of my sin.
—PSALM 32:5

A wise man or woman will never sacrifice
God's best for something that is deceptive—
that promises what it cannot fulfill and only
gives momentary pleasure. Let the
Holy Spirit clean up your life.

DR. CHARLES F. STANLEY

From his sermon,
"The Holy Spirit—His True Identity"
The Power of the Holy Spirit in the Life of the Believer

 "He, when He comes, will convict the world concerning
sin and righteousness and judgment."
—JOHN 16:8

The Holy Spirit helps believers discern between what is true and what is not; what is wise and what is foolish; what is best and what is simply okay.

DR. CHARLES F. STANLEY

From his book,
The Wonderful Spirit-Filled Life

 "When He, the Spirit of truth, comes, He will guide you into all the truth; for He will not speak on His own initiative, but whatever He hears, He will speak; and He will disclose to you what is to come." —JOHN 16:13

There are people who have great talents and abilities—who are eloquent, skilled, organized, and may even come across as being full of the Holy Spirit—but they work in the flesh and fool a lot of people. The work of the Holy Spirit gives lasting, eternal results, and people who are living in the Spirit can detect whether something is accomplished by human talent or by the Spirit. They can identify the presence of God in what is done.

DR. CHARLES F. STANLEY

From his sermon,
"The Holy Spirit—His True Identity"
The Power of the Holy Spirit in the Life of the Believer

 Beloved, do not believe every spirit, but test the spirits to see whether they are from God, because many false prophets have gone out into the world.
—1 JOHN 4:1

Truth is absolutely essential for victory in the life of a believer. If you and I do not know the truth about God, Jesus, the Holy Spirit, ourselves, and our position in Christ, then when Satan attacks us, we're going to be fearful and doubt our relationships with the Lord. And when fear comes upon us, we are already headed for major defeat.

DR. CHARLES F. STANLEY

From his sermon,
"The Armor of God"

Be strong in the Lord and in the strength of His might.... Stand firm therefore, HAVING GIRDED YOUR LOINS WITH TRUTH.
—EPHESIANS 6:10, 14

When I think about the breastplate of righteousness, I think about how God protects us in our emotions. The Lord doesn't want us living on the basis of our feelings. Rather, He wants our lives to be characterized by righteous living—making right decisions and guarding our behavior through the power and guidance of the Holy Spirit.

DR. CHARLES F. STANLEY

From his sermon,
"The Armor of God"

Put on the full armor of God, so that you will be able to stand firm against the schemes of the devil. . . . HAVING PUT ON THE BREASTPLATE OF RIGHTEOUSNESS.
—EPHESIANS 6:11, 14

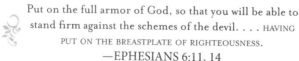

We are to have our feet shod with the preparation of the gospel of peace. That is, we are to stand upon the foundation of the gospel of Jesus Christ. We have been saved by the grace of God and are sealed unto the day of redemption by the Spirit—a firm foundation that is eternally secure. And we should be ready to share our faith and defend what we believe.

DR. CHARLES F. STANLEY

From his sermon,
"The Armor of God"

Having shod YOUR FEET WITH THE PREPARATION OF THE GOSPEL OF PEACE. . . . pray on my behalf, that utterance may be given to me in the opening of my mouth, to make known with boldness the mystery of the gospel. —EPHESIANS 6:15, 19

How do we extinguish all the flaming missiles of the evil one—the spiritual arrows of temptation and trial that Satan sends our way? A very important part of our defense against the Devil is our faith. We believe God. We take Him at His word. We trust that He is our Shield, our Defender. He is the One responsible for diverting Satan's attack upon us, and we have full confidence in Him.

DR. CHARLES F. STANLEY

From his sermon,
"The Armor of God"

 In addition to all this, take up the shield of faith, with which
you can extinguish all the flaming arrows of the evil one.
—EPHESIANS 6:16 NIV

The helmet is . . . a reminder of the presence of the Holy Spirit. The Spirit of Christ dwells in each of us. Just as Christ—through the Spirit—was able to overcome temptation, we, too, have the potential to say no. His presence in us has empowered us to overcome the Devil.

DR. CHARLES F. STANLEY

From his book,
Charles F. Stanley's Handbook for Christian Living

For our struggle is not against flesh and blood, but against the rulers, against the powers, against the world forces of this darkness, against the spiritual forces of wickedness in the heavenly places . . . take THE HELMET OF SALVATION.
—EPHESIANS 6:12, 17

The Word of God is the weapon the
Holy Spirit uses to expose and destroy the lies
confronting the children of God.

DR. CHARLES F. STANLEY

From his book,
The Wonderful Spirit-Filled Life

 Your word I have treasured in my heart, that I
may not sin against You. Blessed are You,
O LORD; teach me Your statutes.
—PSALM 119:11–12

The sword of the Spirit—the Word of God—
is our defense against satanic attacks. When
we face battles, we're not to argue or debate
with the enemy. We simply say, "Here's what
God says." And Scripture teaches that
when we do this, the Devil flees.

DR. CHARLES F. STANLEY

From his sermon,
"The Armor of God"

 Take up the full armor of God, so that you will be able to resist
in the evil day, and having done everything, to stand firm . . .
and take . . . the sword of the Spirit, which is the word of God.
—EPHESIANS 6:13, 17

Not only is the sword of the Spirit defensive, but it is also an offensive weapon. You can sit down with people, share Scripture with them, tell them how to know the Lord Jesus Christ as their personal Savior, and what happens? The gospel can penetrate any darkness, any theological or philosophical defenses, any hardened heart. They get saved because the Spirit testifies that what they've heard is the truth.

DR. CHARLES F. STANLEY

From his sermon,
"The Armor of God"

The word of God is living and active and sharper than any two-edged sword, and piercing as far as the division of soul and spirit, of both joints and marrow, and able to judge the thoughts and intentions of the heart.
—HEBREWS 4:12

There is a spiritual power that comes into a person's life when they humble themselves before God—crying out to the Lord, praying, and talking to the Father. We can stand firm and draw our strength from Him.

DR. CHARLES F. STANLEY

From his sermon,
"The Armor of God"

 With all prayer and petition pray at all times in the Spirit, and with this in view, be on the alert with all perseverance and petition for all the saints.
—EPHESIANS 6:18

When we pray in the Spirit, it means we intercede in absolute submission to God. The Holy Spirit prays through us according to God's will. Don't you want the Spirit to voice through you what He knows needs to be prayed?

DR. CHARLES F. STANLEY

From his sermon,
"The Armor of God"

 He who searches the hearts knows what the mind of the Spirit is, because He intercedes for the saints according to the will of God. —ROMANS 8:27

Spiritual blindness is the inability of a person to understand, perceive, grasp, comprehend, or digest spiritual truth. It is a very dangerous condition. This person is walking in darkness and cannot see where he or she is going.

DR. CHARLES F. STANLEY

From his sermon,
"Spiritual Blindness"

 The god of this world has blinded the minds of the
unbelieving so that they might not see the light of the
gospel of the glory of Christ, who is the image of God.
—2 CORINTHIANS 4:4

The ultimate outcome of spiritual blindness is to be eternally separated from almighty God.

DR. CHARLES F. STANLEY

From his sermon, "Spiritual Blindness"

"I have appeared to you, to appoint you a minister and a witness . . . to open their eyes so that they may turn from darkness to light and from the dominion of Satan to God, that they may receive forgiveness of sins and an inheritance among those who have been sanctified by faith in Me."
—ACTS 26:16, 18

Anything that clashes with what is true is not of the Spirit. . . . Therefore, to walk in the Spirit, we must get serious about guarding our minds.

DR. CHARLES F. STANLEY

From his book,
The Wonderful Spirit-Filled Life

See to it that no one takes you captive through philosophy and empty deception, according to the tradition of men, according to the elementary principles of the world, rather than according to Christ. For in Him all the fullness of Deity dwells in bodily form, and in Him you have been made complete, and He is the head over all rule and authority.
—COLOSSIANS 2:8–10

If a person does not believe the full counsel of God's Word, is not living a godly life, and is not discerning in spirit, then he has no business giving you advice about anything. Apart from the Spirit of God, he cannot counsel you wisely.

DR. CHARLES F. STANLEY

From his sermon,
"The Power of a Discerning Spirit"

 Many plans are in a man's heart, but the counsel of the LORD will stand.
—PROVERBS 19:21

We should always measure our lives against the light and truth of God's Word. Through Scripture, the Holy Spirit can alert us to dangerous trends in our lives or confirm that we're heading in the right direction.

DR. CHARLES F. STANLEY

From
The Charles F. Stanley Life Principles Bible

 If by the Spirit you are putting to death the deeds of the body, you will live. For all who are being led by the Spirit of God, these are sons of God.
—ROMANS 8:13–14

Like almost all of God's gifts to man, the ability to imagine has been corrupted by sin. . . . There is no legitimate place in the mind of the believer for ideas, notions, dreams, or fantasies that have as part of all their content things that are contrary to the truth of God. To entertain such thoughts for even a moment is to set our minds on the flesh and therefore walk after the flesh.

DR. CHARLES F. STANLEY

From his book,
The Wonderful Spirit-Filled Life

We are destroying speculations and every lofty thing raised up against the knowledge of God, and we are taking every thought captive to the obedience of Christ, and we are ready to punish all disobedience.
—2 CORINTHIANS 10:5–6

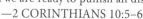

Stay clear of any teacher, preacher, or anyone else who encourages you to do something, read something, or say something to harness the power of the Holy Spirit. The Holy Spirit's power cannot be harnessed. His power cannot be used to accomplish anything other than the Father's will.

DR. CHARLES F. STANLEY

From his book,
The Wonderful Spirit-Filled Life

 No prophecy was ever made by an act of human will, but men moved by the Holy Spirit spoke from God.
—2 PETER 1:21

Men and women who claim to be doing miracles in the power of the Holy Spirit, but who are doing it in such a way to draw attention to the miracle rather than to Christ, are deceivers. Jesus wouldn't have a part of it then, and He will have no part of it now.

DR. CHARLES F. STANLEY

From his book,
The Wonderful Spirit-Filled Life

"False Christs and false prophets will arise, and will show signs and wonders, in order to lead astray, if possible, the elect. But take heed; behold, I have told you everything in advance."
—MARK 13:22–23

We must go beyond evaluating things based on their moral or ethical merit alone. There is more to decision-making for the child of God than that. We must allow the Spirit-filled conscience to discern. Only then can we know what is and what is not of God.

DR. CHARLES F. STANLEY

From his book,
The Wonderful Spirit-Filled Life

 The LORD gives wisdom; from His mouth come knowledge and understanding. He stores up sound wisdom for the upright; He is a shield to those who walk in integrity, guarding the paths of justice, and He preserves the way of His godly ones. Then you will discern righteousness and justice and equity and every good course.
—PROVERBS 2:6–9

I believe the Holy Spirit works in conjunction with the conscience. Where the conscience sends the signal, the Holy Spirit reveals the reason for heeding the alarm. The Spirit urges us and guides us. He reminds us, as the alarm system sounds, that we are accountable to God. Unsaved people have the alarm system, but they don't have the Spirit to explain or guide.

DR. CHARLES F. STANLEY

From his book,
Charles F. Stanley's Handbook for Christian Living

 Pray for us, for we are sure that we have a good conscience, desiring to conduct ourselves honorably in all things.
—HEBREWS 13:18

Remember this: God has put a limit on all adversity. Because you are a child of God, the Holy Spirit is living inside of you, and He knows how much you can bear.

DR. CHARLES F. STANLEY

From
The Charles F. Stanley Life Principles Bible

Just as a father has compassion on his children, so the LORD has compassion on those who fear Him. For He Himself knows our frame; He is mindful that we are but dust.
—PSALM 103:13–14

We live under the protection of the
Holy Spirit; nothing can happen to us
that God does not allow, and we know that
whatever He permits—no matter how bad it
may seem—He can turn for our good.

DR. CHARLES F. STANLEY

From
The Charles F. Stanley Life Principles Bible

 We know that God causes all things to work
together for good to those who love God, to
those who are called according to His purpose.
—ROMANS 8:28

Although you may be facing a situation that makes you feel isolated, helpless, or directionless, understand that you're never alone. The Holy Spirit is with you, to live the life of Christ through you—helping you face every challenge in a godly, victorious manner.

DR. CHARLES F. STANLEY

From
The Charles F. Stanley Life Principles Bible

 The LORD is near to the brokenhearted and saves those who are crushed in spirit. Many are the afflictions of the righteous, but the LORD delivers him out of them all. . . . The LORD redeems the soul of His servants, and none of those who take refuge in Him will be condemned.
—PSALM 34:18–19, 22

The Holy Spirit has never produced a wimp or a failure. Just the opposite is true. Hundreds of believers attribute their success to the changes that took place in their lives once they surrendered to the promptings of the Spirit.

DR. CHARLES F. STANLEY

From his book,
The Wonderful Spirit-Filled Life

 I pray that the eyes of your heart may be enlightened, so that you will know what is the hope of His calling, what are the riches of the glory of His inheritance in the saints, and what is the surpassing greatness of His power toward us who believe.
—EPHESIANS 1:18–19

HOW HE TRANSFORMS US

Conforming Us to the
Likeness of Christ

*Those whom He foreknew, He also predestined to become
conformed to the image of His Son, so that He would be
the firstborn among many brethren.*

—ROMANS 8:29

The best picture of what a
Spirit-filled man looks
like is Christ.

DR. CHARLES F. STANLEY

From his book,
The Wonderful Spirit-Filled Life

 I want to know Christ and the power of his resurrection and the
fellowship of sharing in his sufferings, becoming like him in his
death, and so, somehow, to attain to the resurrection from the dead.
—PHILIPPIANS 3:10–11 NIV

Jesus, who lived such a remarkable life, has sent His Spirit to dwell in you. His goal is to reproduce Himself through you—the courage, the self-control, the love, everything.

DR. CHARLES F. STANLEY

From his book,
The Wonderful Spirit-Filled Life

 Be renewed in the spirit of your mind, and put on the new self, which in the likeness of God has been created in righteousness and holiness of the truth.
—EPHESIANS 4:23–24

Our response pattern to life is deeply rooted in our personality and our character. Only the Holy Spirit can change our perspective on life, our response to life, and our evaluation of life.

DR. CHARLES F. STANLEY

From his book,
Living in the Power of the Holy Spirit

You have taken off your old self with its practices and have put on the new self, which is being renewed in knowledge in the image of its Creator.
—COLOSSIANS 3:9–10 NIV

Learning to recognize the Holy Spirit
is the first step in learning to live
the Spirit-filled life.

DR. CHARLES F. STANLEY

From his book,
The Wonderful Spirit-Filled Life

The Spirit of the LORD will rest on Him, the spirit of wisdom and
understanding, the spirit of counsel and strength, the spirit of knowledge
and the fear of the LORD. And He will delight in the fear of the LORD,
and He will not judge by what His eyes see, nor make a decision by what
His ears hear; but with righteousness He will judge.
—ISAIAH 11:2–4

As you obey the promptings of the Spirit,
you will begin to see spiritual realities that
only a person who is in constant communion
with the Father can perceive.

DR. CHARLES F. STANLEY

From his book,
The Ultimate Conversation

Who is the man who fears the LORD? He will instruct him in the
way he should choose. . . . The secret of the LORD is for those
who fear Him, and He will make them know His covenant.
—PSALM 25:12, 14

I'm not saying that yielding to the will of the Father is easy—not at all. But it is absolutely required. If the Holy Spirit is going to prevail in my life, I have to give Him control.

DR. CHARLES F. STANLEY

From his sermon,
"The Holy Spirit—An Absolute Essential"

"GOD IS OPPOSED TO THE PROUD, BUT GIVES GRACE TO THE HUMBLE." Submit therefore to God. Resist the devil and he will flee from you. —JAMES 4:6–7

If walking in the Spirit is a matter of walking in the truth, then memorizing Scripture and meditating on it are the best things you can do to facilitate that walk. The more familiar you are with truth, the easier it will be to recognize error.

DR. CHARLES F. STANLEY

From his book,
The Wonderful Spirit-Filled Life

 "This book of the law shall not depart from your mouth, but you shall meditate on it day and night, so that you may be careful to do according to all that is written in it; for then you will make your way prosperous, and then you will have success."
—JOSHUA 1:8

Whereas before you had a general sense of right and wrong, the Holy Spirit began renewing your mind to more specific and complete truths. . . . You participate in this renewal process every time you read your Bible, attend worship, memorize a verse, or pray.

DR. CHARLES F. STANLEY

From his book,
The Wonderful Spirit-Filled Life

 Do not be conformed to this world, but be transformed by the renewing of your mind, so that you may prove what the will of God is, that which is good and acceptable and perfect. —ROMANS 12:2

The Holy Spirit will never
lead you where the Word of God
forbids you to go.

DR. CHARLES F. STANLEY

From his book,
The Wonderful Spirit-Filled Life

 As for God, His way is blameless; the word of the LORD
is tried; He is a shield to all who take refuge in Him.
—PSALM 18:30

It wasn't enough for the Holy Spirit to inspire men to write the Bible. He knew each of us would need someone to lead us through the text as well. So every time a believer opens his or her Bible, the Spirit goes to work to illuminate the Scriptures. In that way, He is able to minister to each of us, at the right pace, according to our particular needs.

DR. CHARLES F. STANLEY

From his book,
The Wonderful Spirit–Filled Life

Whatever was written in earlier times was written for our instruction, so that through perseverance and the encouragement of the Scriptures we might have hope.
—ROMANS 15:4

Dependence on God is not weakness.
No! It takes a strong man or a strong
woman to rely upon the Holy Spirit.

DR. CHARLES F. STANLEY

From his sermon,
"The Holy Spirit—An Absolute Essential"

"Be strong and courageous! Do not tremble or be dismayed,
for the LORD your God is with you wherever you go."
—JOSHUA 1:9

Yieldedness and brokenness
[clears] the way for the Holy Spirit
to take control.

DR. CHARLES F. STANLEY

From his book,
The Wonderful Spirit-Filled Life

We were burdened excessively, beyond our strength, so that we despaired
even of life; indeed, we had the sentence of death within ourselves so
that we would not trust in ourselves, but in God who raises the dead;
who delivered us from so great a peril of death, and will deliver us, He
on whom we have set our hope. And He will yet deliver us.
—2 CORINTHIANS 1:8–10

What can stop this work of the Holy Spirit in our lives? Only one thing—our refusal to allow Him to work in us. Once we are born again spiritually, we cannot remove the Holy Spirit from our lives, but we can willfully choose not to respond to Him as He seeks to lead and guide us daily.

DR. CHARLES F. STANLEY

From his book,
Living in the Power of the Holy Spirit

Do not quench the Spirit; do not despise prophetic utterances. But examine everything carefully; hold fast to that which is good; abstain from every form of evil.
—1 THESSALONIANS 5:19–22

More people discover the wonderful Spirit-filled life in the valley than in any other place. God uses sickness, financial pressure, appetites, habits, children, work, whatever it takes. Because once He finally has our attention, He knows the best is yet to come.

DR. CHARLES F. STANLEY

From his book,
The Wonderful Spirit-Filled Life

Although the Lord has given you bread of privation and water of oppression, He, your Teacher will no longer hide Himself, but your eyes will behold your Teacher. Your ears will hear a word behind you, "This is the way, walk in it," whenever you turn to the right or to the left.
—ISAIAH 30:20–21

Every time you and I make a decision, our choice determines whether we remain filled with the Holy Spirit or not. The Spirit of God cannot be in control as long as I demand my own way.

DR. CHARLES F. STANLEY

From his sermon,
"The Holy Spirit—An Absolute Essential"

 Those who live according to the sinful nature have their minds set on what that nature desires; but those who live in accordance with the Spirit have their minds set on what the Spirit desires.
—ROMANS 8:5 NIV

We know that Christ was raised from the dead, and we've been promised that our mortal bodies will be raised as He was. God resurrects our physical bodies to take them home in their transformed condition to heaven. That is the work of the Holy Spirit— changing our bodies from natural and perishable to eternal.

DR. CHARLES F. STANLEY

From his sermon,
"The Holy Spirit—His True Identity"
The Power of the Holy Spirit in the Life of the Believer

If the Spirit of Him who raised Jesus from the dead dwells in you, He who raised Christ Jesus from the dead will also give life to your mortal bodies through His Spirit who dwells in you.
—ROMANS 8:11

Surrendered men and women who have given over control of their lives to the Savior welcome the Father's will. They are not afraid of the Spirit's leading.

DR. CHARLES F. STANLEY

From his book,
The Wonderful Spirit-Filled Life

 There is no fear in love; but perfect love casts out fear, because fear involves punishment, and the one who fears is not perfected in love.
—1 JOHN 4:18

Purity of life and the power of the
Holy Spirit go hand in hand. You cannot
separate the two. You cannot have the fullness
or the power of the Holy Spirit exercised
through you when you're living in sin.

DR. CHARLES F. STANLEY

From his sermon,
"The Holy Spirit—His True Identity"
The Power of the Holy Spirit in the Life of the Believer

 The flesh sets its desire against the Spirit, and the Spirit
against the flesh; for these are in opposition to one another,
so that you may not do the things that you please. But if you
are led by the Spirit, you are not under the Law.
—GALATIANS 5:17–18

Pastors who are filled with the Spirit don't simply use the pulpit to entertain and comfort their people. . . . They equip and challenge their congregation to do the work of the ministry. And they teach and model how God's work can be done in His strength.

DR. CHARLES F. STANLEY

From his book,
The Wonderful Spirit-Filled Life

Brethren, whatever is true, whatever is honorable, whatever is right, whatever is pure, whatever is lovely, whatever is of good repute, if there is any excellence and if anything worthy of praise, dwell on these things. The things you have learned and received and heard and seen in me, practice these things, and the God of peace will be with you.
—PHILIPPIANS 4:8–9

Walking in the Spirit is not a solo mission. It is not an excuse for you to become isolated from other Christians. A believer who pulls away from the body to do his or her own "spiritual" thing is not walking in the Spirit. You can't walk in the Spirit apart from functioning in the body of Christ. It won't work. It has never worked.

DR. CHARLES F. STANLEY

From his book,
Charles F. Stanley's Handbook for Christian Living

Let us consider how to stimulate one another to love and good deeds, not forsaking our own assembling together, as is the habit of some, but encouraging one another; and all the more as you see the day drawing near.
—HEBREWS 10:24–25

The Spirit-filled life is a life of faith. . . .
The Spirit-filled life is not a formula; it
is a relationship, a relationship with a
Person—the Holy Spirit.

DR. CHARLES F. STANLEY

From his book,
The Wonderful Spirit-Filled Life

 We are the true circumcision, who worship in the Spirit of God
and glory in Christ Jesus and put no confidence in the flesh.
—PHILIPPIANS 3:3

Once a person becomes a child of God,
the conscience takes on new significance.
It becomes a divine tool. It functions as a
megaphone in the hands of the Holy Spirit.
It becomes the means through which the
Holy Spirit reveals the will of God to the mind.

DR. CHARLES F. STANLEY

From his book,
The Wonderful Spirit-Filled Life

Our proud confidence is this: the testimony of our
conscience, that in holiness and godly sincerity, not in
fleshly wisdom but in the grace of God, we have conducted
ourselves in the world, and especially toward you.
—2 CORINTHIANS 1:12

The work of the Holy Spirit is to train us, sift and sand us, chip away at things that are foreign to the family we belong to. As any father who loves his children does, our heavenly Father meets our needs, but He doesn't stop there. He is also our trainer, giving us guidance. When we don't respond to the gentle taps on the shoulder, He will use hardship, failure, and even [the consequences of] our sin to bring our behavior in line with His holiness.

DR. CHARLES F. STANLEY

From his book,
Charles F. Stanley's Handbook for Christian Living

 Create in me a clean heart, O God, and renew a steadfast spirit within me. Do not cast me away from Your presence and do not take Your Holy Spirit from me. Restore to me the joy of Your salvation and sustain me with a willing spirit. Then I will teach transgressors Your ways, and sinners will be converted to You.
—PSALM 51:10–13

Everywhere you turn, the Spirit of God is working in your life—bringing you from stagnation to growth, from emptiness to joy, from failure to success. The Holy Spirit is moving you in a direction that brings glory to the Father.

DR. CHARLES F. STANLEY

From his sermon,
"The Holy Spirit—An Absolute Essential"

As you have received Christ Jesus the Lord, so walk in Him, having been firmly rooted and now being built up in Him and established in your faith, just as you were instructed, and overflowing with gratitude.
—COLOSSIANS 2:6–7

We [are] never going to find out what [pleases] the Holy Spirit until we [care] more about hearing from Him than we [do] about getting our way.

DR. CHARLES F. STANLEY

From his book,
The Wonderful Spirit-Filled Life

You who say, "Today or tomorrow we will go to such and such a city, and spend a year there and engage in business and make a profit." Yet you do not know what your life will be like tomorrow. You are just a vapor that appears for a little while and then vanishes away. Instead, you ought to say, "If the Lord wills, we will live and also do this or that."
—JAMES 4:13–15

I had been consumed with a desire to do something, to somehow win the Holy Spirit. I had been trying to convince God with my sincerity. . . . [But] I had missed the obvious. I had been looking all over for something that was right in front of me. I didn't need to beg. God wanted [the Spirit-filled life] for me more than I wanted it for myself. All I needed to do was believe and move out in faith.

DR. CHARLES F. STANLEY

From his book,
The Wonderful Spirit-Filled Life

 We walk by faith,
not by sight.
—2 CORINTHIANS 5:7

WHEN HE WORKS THROUGH US

Bearing Eternal Fruit

"The seed in the good soil, these are the ones who have heard the word in an honest and good heart, and hold it fast, and bear fruit with perseverance."
—LUKE 8:15

To walk by the Spirit is to live with moment-by-moment dependency on and sensitivity to the initial promptings of the Holy Spirit.

DR. CHARLES F. STANLEY

From his book,
The Wonderful Spirit-Filled Life

 If we live by the Spirit,
let us also walk by the Spirit.
—GALATIANS 5:25

God is looking for imperfect men and women who have learned to walk in moment-by-moment dependence on the Holy Spirit. Christians who have come to terms with their inadequacies, fears, and failures. Believers who have become discontent with "surviving" and have taken time to investigate everything God has to offer in this life.

DR. CHARLES F. STANLEY

From his book,
The Wonderful Spirit–Filled Life

I count all things to be loss in view of the surpassing value of knowing Christ Jesus my Lord, for whom I have suffered the loss of all things, and count them but rubbish so that I may gain Christ.
—PHILIPPIANS 3:8

The people who do God's work God's way don't wait until their efforts fail before they begin trusting Him. They begin their projects as dependent people. And in most cases, they maintain their dependent spirits until the end.

DR. CHARLES F. STANLEY

From his book,
The Wonderful Spirit-Filled Life

Neither the one who plants nor the one who waters is anything, but God who causes the growth. Now he who plants and he who waters are one; but each will receive his own reward according to his own labor. For we are God's fellow workers; you are God's field, God's building.
—1 CORINTHIANS 3:7–9

Baptism is an act of obedience that is absolutely mandatory—not to be saved but to be obedient to God. If you've never been baptized because you don't think it's necessary, realize that you cannot be filled with the Holy Spirit because you're willfully disobeying a specific, clear command of Jesus Christ.

DR. CHARLES F. STANLEY

From his sermon,
"The Holy Spirit—His True Identity"
The Power of the Holy Spirit in the Life of the Believer

We have been buried with Him through baptism into death, so that as Christ was raised from the dead through the glory of the Father, so we too might walk in newness of life.
—ROMANS 6:4

The Spirit-filled life begins when we are absolutely and thoroughly convinced that we can do nothing apart from the indwelling strength of the Holy Spirit.

DR. CHARLES F. STANLEY

From his book,
The Wonderful Spirit-Filled Life

Not that we are adequate in ourselves to consider anything as coming from ourselves, but our adequacy is from God, who also made us adequate as servants of a new covenant, not of the letter but of the Spirit; for the letter kills, but the Spirit gives life.
—2 CORINTHIANS 3:5–6

Spirit-filled believers are given to prayer.

DR. CHARLES F. STANLEY

From his book,
The Wonderful Spirit-Filled Life

Devote yourselves to prayer, keeping alert in it with an
attitude of thanksgiving; praying at the same time for us as
well, that God will open up to us a door for the word, so
that we may speak forth the mystery of Christ.
—COLOSSIANS 4:2–3

The person who is filled with the
Holy Spirit is going to be a person of
generous, joyful, and overflowing
praise and thanksgiving to God.

DR. CHARLES F. STANLEY

From his book,
Living in the Power of the Holy Spirit

Be filled with the Spirit, speaking to one another in psalms and
hymns and spiritual songs, singing and making melody with
your heart to the Lord; always giving thanks for all things in the
name of our Lord Jesus Christ to God, even the Father.
—EPHESIANS 5:18–20

The Holy Spirit enables us to live truly
changed, dynamic, and vibrant lives so that
others will want to know the source of
our joy, peace, and confidence.

DR. CHARLES F. STANLEY

From his book,
Living in the Power of the Holy Spirit

Sanctify Christ as Lord in your hearts, always being ready to
make a defense to everyone who asks you to give an account for
the hope that is in you, yet with gentleness and reverence.
—1 PETER 3:15

It doesn't matter whether your testimony is simple or dramatic. If Jesus is the center of attention, it will sow the seed that the Holy Spirit will nourish into life. Your witness—your testimony—can mean the difference between heaven and hell for others.

DR. CHARLES F. STANLEY

From his book,
Charles F. Stanley's Handbook for Christian Living

When I came to you, brethren, I did not come with superiority of speech or of wisdom, proclaiming to you the testimony of God. For I determined to know nothing among you except Jesus Christ, and Him crucified.
—1 CORINTHIANS 2:1–2

The genuinely Spirit-filled person will not be calloused toward others, careless or slothful in work, indifferent in responsibility, or satisfied with mediocrity.

DR. CHARLES F. STANLEY

From his book,
Living in the Power of the Holy Spirit

This is His commandment, that we believe in the name of His Son Jesus Christ, and love one another, just as He commanded us. The one who keeps His commandments abides in Him, and He in him. We know by this that He abides in us, by the Spirit whom He has given us.
—1 JOHN 3:23–24

The Spirit-filled person is going to be so filled with love for God and others, and so willing to trust God to work in his own life and in the lives of others, that he will be willing to submit to others rather than demand his own way.

DR. CHARLES F. STANLEY

From his book,
Living in the Power of the Holy Spirit

 Be subject to one another
in the fear of Christ.
—EPHESIANS 5:21

Those who are filled with the Holy Spirit have a bearing of authority about them—they often bear the marks of spiritual leadership.

DR. CHARLES F. STANLEY

From his book,
Living in the Power of the Holy Spirit

 They were amazed at His teaching; for He was teaching them as one having authority.
—MARK 1:22

A clear conscience is evidence
of a life in harmony with
the Holy Spirit.

DR. CHARLES F. STANLEY

From his book,
The Wonderful Spirit-Filled Life

 Fight the good fight, keeping faith and a good conscience, which
some have rejected and suffered shipwreck in regard to their faith.
—1 TIMOTHY 1:18–19

It is Christ's life pouring into us that enables us to live the Christian life and to bear the hallmarks of character that we call the fruit of the Spirit.

DR. CHARLES F. STANLEY

From his book,
Living in the Power of the Holy Spirit

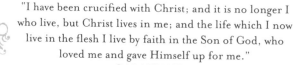

"I have been crucified with Christ; and it is no longer I who live, but Christ lives in me; and the life which I now live in the flesh I live by faith in the Son of God, who loved me and gave Himself up for me."
—GALATIANS 2:20

This is the will of God: That He can reveal Himself in and through you as a result of the Holy Spirit living within you. This means that from you flows love, joy, peace, patience, kindness, goodness, faithfulness, gentleness, and self-control—all the fruit of the Spirit that demonstrates His character.

DR. CHARLES F. STANLEY

From his sermon,
"Our Constant Companion"

 "My Father is glorified by this, that you bear much fruit, and so prove to be My disciples."
—JOHN 15:8

Our embodiment of the Holy Spirit's nature is our greatest witness. Our expressions and words of love, joy, and peace are what draw others to us so they want to hear the gospel.

DR. CHARLES F. STANLEY

From his book,
Living in the Power of the Holy Spirit

"Let your light shine before men in such a way that they may see your good works, and glorify your Father who is in heaven."
—MATTHEW 5:16

As believers, our potential for righteous living is in direct proportion to our willingness to allow the Holy Spirit to produce His fruit through us.

DR. CHARLES F. STANLEY

From his book,
The Wonderful Spirit–Filled Life

"Blessed is the man who trusts in the LORD and whose trust is the LORD. For he will be like a tree planted by the water, that extends its roots by a stream and will not fear when the heat comes; but its leaves will be green, and it will not be anxious in a year of drought nor cease to yield fruit."
—JEREMIAH 17:7–8

The fruit of the Spirit is not environmentally sensitive. It's one thing to have peace and joy when everything is going your way. It's another thing altogether to maintain your peace and joy when the bottom falls out.

DR. CHARLES F. STANLEY

From his book,
The Wonderful Spirit–Filled Life

We do not lose heart, but though our outer man is decaying, yet our inner man is being renewed day by day. For momentary, light affliction is producing for us an eternal weight of glory far beyond all comparison, while we look not at the things which are seen, but at the things which are not seen; for the things which are seen are temporal, but the things which are not seen are eternal.
—2 CORINTHIANS 4:16–18

Whereas the gifts of the Spirit are for building up the body . . . the fruit of the Spirit is the fragrance that invites nonbelievers to become members of the body.

DR. CHARLES F. STANLEY

From his book,
The Wonderful Spirit–Filled Life

We are a fragrance of Christ to God among those who are being saved and among those who are perishing; to the one an aroma from death to death, to the other an aroma from life to life.
—2 CORINTHIANS 2:15–16

There is no such thing
as a non-gifted believer.

DR. CHARLES F. STANLEY

From his sermon,
"The Holy Spirit—An Absolute Essential"

 The gifts and the calling
of God are irrevocable.
—ROMANS 11:29

Through the Holy Spirit, who has gifted you with your personality, your talents, your background, the circumstances of your birth, and all of that—God fused the work He has called you to do into your being even before you were born. And the Holy Spirit enables you to carry it out.

DR. CHARLES F. STANLEY

From his sermon,
"The Holy Spirit—An Absolute Essential"

 We are His workmanship, created in Christ Jesus for good works, which God prepared beforehand so that we would walk in them. —EPHESIANS 2:10

When you take a person, put him in his spiritual gift, and help him understand how to operate out of that gift, you're going to see a person who begins to reach toward the maximum of his potential—a person who fulfills God's purpose for His life.

DR. CHARLES F. STANLEY

From his sermon,
"The Holy Spirit—An Absolute Essential"

 Do not neglect the spiritual gift within you . . .
Take pains with these things; be absorbed in them,
so that your progress will be evident to all.
—1 TIMOTHY 4:14–15

When you and I operate out of our spiritual gifts, we do our best. We have our greatest sense of fulfillment, accomplishment, and achievement in life. And not only are we productive, but we are also impactful.

DR. CHARLES F. STANLEY

From his sermon,
"The Gift of Prophecy"
Living in the Power of the Holy Spirit

Fan into flame the gift of God, which is in you through the laying on of my hands. For God did not give us a spirit of timidity, but a spirit of power, of love and of self-discipline.
—2 TIMOTHY 1:6–7 NIV

Through the distributing and networking of spiritual gifts, God has created a system ensuring (1) that every believer has a significant role in the body of Christ and (2) that believers work together to accomplish His overall purpose.

DR. CHARLES F. STANLEY

From his book,
The Wonderful Spirit–Filled Life

 There are varieties of effects, but the same God who works all things in all persons. But to each one is given the manifestation of the Spirit for the common good. —1 CORINTHIANS 12:6–7

God never contradicts Himself as He
gives each member of His body commands,
so when everyone is faithfully submitted to
His will, we are all working toward
the same goal—to glorify Him and
lead others to salvation.

DR. CHARLES F. STANLEY

From
The Charles F. Stanley Life Principles Bible

 There are varieties of gifts, but the same Spirit. And
there are varieties of ministries, and the same Lord.
—1 CORINTHIANS 12:4–5

When the Holy Spirit works through
people with the spiritual gift of prophecy, He
roots them in the truth and fills them with a
passion for God's Word. They usually make
wonderful friends because they are generally
very loyal, will help you confront areas of
spiritual weakness, and are
very understandable and persuasive
when teaching the truth.

DR. CHARLES F. STANLEY

From his sermon,
"The Gift of Prophecy"
Living in the Power of the Holy Spirit

Follow the way of love and eagerly desire
spiritual gifts, especially the gift of prophecy.
—1 CORINTHIANS 14:1 NIV

People who exercise the gift of service
are practicing one of the most important
principles of success in life: Give yourself
away to help others accomplish their
goals, and God will bless you.

DR. CHARLES F. STANLEY

From his sermon,
"The Gift of Service"
Living in the Power of the Holy Spirit

Each one should use whatever gift he has received to serve others,
faithfully administering God's grace in its various forms. . . . If
anyone serves, he should do it with the strength God provides,
so that in all things God may be praised through Jesus Christ. To
him be the glory and the power for ever and ever. Amen.
—1 PETER 4:10–11 NIV

Those with the gift of teaching who are walking in the Spirit get joy and fulfillment out of studying the Word, but they are also wired to share what they've learned with others. Why? It's not enough for them to impart their knowledge—they desire to see God transform people's lives. They want Him to speak to people's hearts.

DR. CHARLES F. STANLEY

From his sermon,
"The Gift of Teaching"
Living in the Power of the Holy Spirit

 We proclaim Him, admonishing every man and teaching every man with all wisdom, so that we may present every man complete in Christ.
—COLOSSIANS 1:28

Individuals with the gift of exhortation are committed to helping others grow spiritually and accomplishing the purposes God planned for them. They can see potential and possibilities in others—how the Father can work in their lives—so they're motivated to encourage others to become the people God created them to be.

DR. CHARLES F. STANLEY

From his sermon,
"The Gift of Exhortation"
Living in the Power of the Holy Spirit

Brethren, we request and exhort you in the Lord Jesus, that as you received from us instruction as to how you ought to walk and please God (just as you actually do walk), that you excel still more.
—1 THESSALONIANS 4:1

What brings the greatest satisfaction to people with the spiritual gift of giving is obeying God when He reveals a need to them. They know they can't outgive God and that He always provides exactly what they need—so money isn't the issue. They can give in secret and not need applause or recognition, because they just want to please the Father. And God always honors that.

DR. CHARLES F. STANLEY

From his sermon,
"The Gift of Giving"
Living in the Power of the Holy Spirit

Each one must do just as he has purposed in his heart, not grudgingly or under compulsion, for God loves a cheerful giver. And God is able to make all grace abound to you, so that always having all sufficiency in everything, you may have an abundance for every good deed.
—2 CORINTHIANS 9:7–8

When you're willing to ask God for His wisdom—when you accept His unconditional love to enable you and trust in His power to provide for you—you can accomplish everything the Lord has planned for your life. The person with the spiritual gift of organization is wired to function this way. They're motivated to achieve God's objectives—to take major goals and break them up into achievable tasks. They understand the big picture, visualize the end results, and always experience great joy when seeing the plan accomplished.

DR. CHARLES F. STANLEY

From his sermon,
"The Gift of Exhortation"
Living in the Power of the Holy Spirit

 The administration of this service not only supplies the needs of the saints, but also is abounding through many thanksgivings to God.
—2 CORINTHIANS 9:12 NKJV

People who are blessed with the spiritual gift of mercy do not live by their feelings, but are very sensitive to other people's emotions. They understand people who are in distress and have a deep desire to comfort them. God can work through them to heal others.

DR. CHARLES F. STANLEY

From his sermon,
"The Gift of Mercy"
Living in the Power of the Holy Spirit

 We have different gifts, according to the grace given to each of us. If your gift is . . . to show mercy, do it cheerfully. —ROMANS 12:6, 8 NIV

You show me any man or woman who is filled with the Spirit, relying upon the Holy Spirit, and operating out of his or her spiritual gift, and I'll show you someone who is going to get ahead in life, and who will be successful in what they're doing.

DR. CHARLES F. STANLEY

From his sermon,
"The Holy Spirit—An Absolute Essential"

 Thanks be to God, who always leads us in triumph in Christ, and manifests through us the sweet aroma of the knowledge of Him in every place.
—2 CORINTHIANS 2:14

When we minister to others through our gifts, we are tapping into the inexhaustible energy and motivation of God. . . . The Holy Spirit flows through us like at no other time.

DR. CHARLES F. STANLEY

From his book,
The Wonderful Spirit-Filled Life

 Since you are zealous of spiritual gifts, seek to abound for the edification of the church.
—1 CORINTHIANS 14:12

Is it possible for someone to walk in the Spirit without exercising her gift? Absolutely not. The Holy Spirit will reveal Himself in a special way through you, through the exercise of your gift. To refuse to use your gift is to say no to the Holy Spirit.

DR. CHARLES F. STANLEY

From his book,
Charles F. Stanley's Handbook for Christian Living

 He gave some as apostles, and some as prophets, and some as evangelists, and some as pastors and teachers, for the equipping of the saints for the work of service, to the building up of the body of Christ; until we all attain to the unity of the faith, and of the knowledge of the Son of God, to a mature man, to the measure of the stature which belongs to the fullness of Christ.
—EPHESIANS 4:11–13

The Holy Spirit has already been poured in. . . . You have all of Him you are ever going to get. The question is, How much of you does He have?

DR. CHARLES F. STANLEY

From his book,
The Wonderful Spirit-Filled Life

 My dear brothers, stand firm. Let nothing move you. Always give yourselves fully to the work of the Lord, because you know that your labor in the Lord is not in vain.
—1 CORINTHIANS 15:58 NIV

The Spirit is calling out to us to carry out the ministry God has given us. His responsibility is to prepare the Body of Christ—sending us out, motivating us, and empowering us to do the work of getting this world ready for the Lord Jesus to return.

DR. CHARLES F. STANLEY

From his sermon,
"The Three Finalities of the Revelation"
Revelation

 The Spirit and the bride say, "Come." And let the one who hears say, "Come." And let the one who is thirsty come; let the one who wishes take the water of life without cost.
—REVELATION 22:17